Time Travel History

EXPLORERS & PIONEERS

Past & Present

BY: SARAH JANISSE BROWN

PORTRAITS BY: SAVANNAH GERDES
DRAWINGS BY: SERGE ANDREEV

Edited By Sue Gerdes & Hannah Corey

The Thinking Tree, LLC

FUNSCHOOLING.COM

ABOUT THIS TIME TRAVEL WORLD HISTORY JOURNAL

Throughout history Explorers and Pioneers have transformed the world. Students will research over 30 different historical figures from throughout the world and the ages. We have chosen to focus on a diverse assortment of men and women who made an impact on the world through their discovery, exploration and pioneering efforts. Students will learn about the accomplishments, family, life, beliefs, and adventures of each influencer.

Dive into thinking about these explorers and pioneers in a way no other material out there does. It is a wonderful way to study history that is fun and engaging. Use daily for a unit lasting about 6 weeks, or weekly to last all year. You can even use this over a period of several years as you study different historical periods. The individuals are presented in this book in alphabetical order, use the book from cover to cover or skip around to research each person in chronological order.

Thinking Tree Learning Levels: C1 & C2, ideal for ages 10+. This journal is an excellent companion to our Make Your Own Timeline of World History and Heroes & Villains of History.

This book uses the Dyslexie font for easier reading for Dyslexic students.

"If I can create the minimum of my plans and desires, there shall be no regrets." – Bessie Coleman

"Everything was so new – the whole idea of going into space was new and daring. There were no textbooks, so we had to write them."

Katherine Johnson

NAME & DATE:____

CONTACT INFORMATION:________________________________

"When something is important enough, you do it even if the odds are not in your favor."

Elon Musk

EXPLORERS & PIONEERS
PAST & PRESENT

Presented in Alphabetical Order

"Don't let anyone rob you of your imagination, your creativity, or your curiosity. It's your place in the world; it's your life. Go on and do all you can with it, and make it the life you want to live." – Mae Jemison

70 Katherine Johnson

74 Gerlinde Kaltenbrunner

78 Christina Koch

82 Meriwether Lewis

86 Ferdinand Magellan

90 Jessica Meir

94 KT Miller

98 Elon Musk

102 Sunita Pandya

106 Francisco Pizarro

110 Jean Baptiste Pointe Du Sable

114 Juan Ponce De Leon

118 Sacagawea

122 Hernando De Soto

128 Amerigo Vespucci

VASCO NUNEZ DE BALBOA

It's Research Time!

Using Internet search, Wikipedia, documentaries or library

Date and place of birth:

What was (or is) his job?

What were (or are) his goals?

What challenges did he face along the way?

Who or what motivated him to accomplish what he did?

Name some of his most notable accomplishments or discoveries:

What is this person most known for:

How would the world be different if he had never been born?

Greatest Explorations:

Design a postage stamp to commemorate this person

Greatest Discoveries:

JEANNE BARET

It's Research Time!

Using Internet search, Wikipedia, documentaries or library

Date and place of birth:

What was (or is) her job?

What were (or are) her goals?

What was her main goal?

In what ways did her life affect our world?

What is this person most known for:

How would the world be different if she had never been born?

Greatest Explorations:

Design a postage stamp to commemorate this person

Greatest Discoveries:

JAMES BECKWOURTH

It's Research Time!

Using Internet search, Wikipedia, documentaries or library

Date and place of birth:

What was (or is) his job?

What were (or are) his goals?

What challenges did he face along the way?

Who or what motivated him to accomplish what he did?

Name some of his most notable accomplishments or discoveries:

What is this person most known for:

How would the world be different if he had never been born?

Greatest Explorations:

Design a postage stamp to commemorate this person

Greatest Discoveries:

JOHN CABOT

It's Research Time!

Using Internet search, Wikipedia, documentaries or library

Date and place of birth:

What was (or is) his job?

What were (or are) his goals?

What challenges did he face along the way?

Who or what motivated him to accomplish what he did?

Name some of his most notable accomplishments or discoveries:

What is this person most known for:

How would the world be different if he had never been born?

Greatest Explorations:

Design a postage stamp to commemorate this person

Greatest Discoveries:

SAMUEL DE CHAMPLAIN

It's Research Time!

Using Internet search, Wikipedia, documentaries or library

Date and place of birth:

What was (or is) his job?

What were (or are) his goals?

What challenges did he face along the way?

Who or what motivated him to accomplish what he did?

Name some of his most notable accomplishments or discoveries:

What is this person most known for:

How would the world be different if he had never been born?

Greatest Explorations:

Design a postage stamp to commemorate this person

Greatest Discoveries:

JACQUES CARTIER

It's Research Time!

Using Internet search, Wikipedia, documentaries or library

Date and place of birth:

What was (or is) his job?

What were (or are) his goals?

What challenges did he face along the way?

Who or what motivated him to accomplish what he did?

Name some of his most notable accomplishments or discoveries:

What is this person most known for:

How would the world be different if he had never been born?

Greatest Explorations:

Design a postage stamp to commemorate this person

Greatest Discoveries:

BESSIE COLEMAN

It's Research Time!

Using Internet search, Wikipedia, documentaries or library

Date and place of birth:

What was (or is) her job?

What were (or are) her goals?

What was her main goal?

In what ways did her life affect our world?

What is this person most known for:

How would the world be different if she had never been born?

Greatest Explorations:

Design a postage stamp to commemorate this person

Greatest Discoveries:

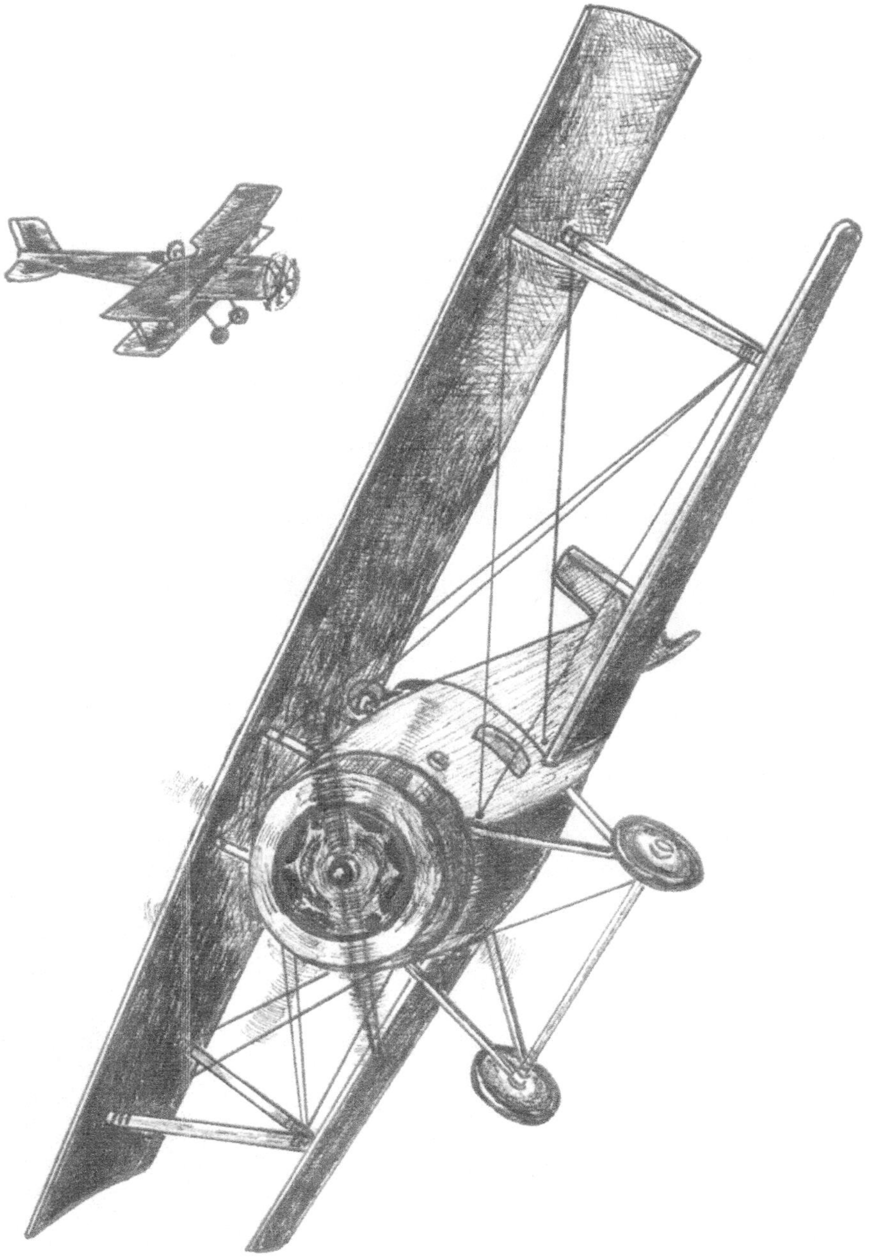

LIEUT. WILLIAM CLARK

It's Research Time!

Using Internet search, Wikipedia, documentaries or library

Date and place of birth:

What was (or is) his job?

What were (or are) his goals?

What challenges did he face along the way?

Who or what motivated him to accomplish what he did?

Name some of his most notable accomplishments or discoveries:

What is this person most known for:

How would the world be different if he had never been born?

Greatest Explorations:

Design a postage stamp to commemorate this person

Greatest Discoveries:

FRANKLIN CHANG DIAZ

It's Research Time!

Using Internet search, Wikipedia, documentaries or library

Date and place of birth:

What was (or is) his job?

What were (or are) his goals?

What challenges did he face along the way?

Who or what motivated him to accomplish what he did?

Name some of his most notable accomplishments or discoveries:

What is this person most known for:

How would the world be different if he had never been born?

Greatest Explorations:

Design a postage stamp to commemorate this person

Greatest Discoveries:

SIR FRANCIS DRAKE

It's Research Time!

Using Internet search, Wikipedia, documentaries or library

Date and place of birth:

What was (or is) his job?

What were (or are) his goals?

What challenges did he face along the way?

Who or what motivated him to accomplish what he did?

Name some of his most notable accomplishments or discoveries:

What is this person most known for:

How would the world be different if he had never been born?

Greatest Explorations:

Design a postage stamp to commemorate this person

Greatest Discoveries:

SYLVIA EARLE

It's Research Time!

Using Internet search, Wikipedia, documentaries or library

Date and place of birth:

What was (or is) her job?

What were (or are) her goals?

What was her main goal?

In what ways did her life affect our world?

What is this person most known for:

How would the world be different if she had never been born?

Greatest Explorations:

Design a postage stamp to commemorate this person

Greatest Discoveries:

VASCO DA GAMA

It's Research Time!

Using Internet search, Wikipedia, documentaries or library

Date and place of birth:

What was (or is) his job?

What were (or are) his goals?

What challenges did he face along the way?

Who or what motivated him to accomplish what he did?

Name some of his most notable accomplishments or discoveries:

What is this person most known for:

How would the world be different if he had never been born?

Greatest Explorations:

Design a postage stamp to commemorate this person

Greatest Discoveries:

JUAN GARRIDO

It's Research Time!

Using Internet search, Wikipedia, documentaries or library

Date and place of birth:

What was (or is) his job?

What were (or are) his goals?

What challenges did he face along the way?

Who or what motivated him to accomplish what he did?

Name some of his most notable accomplishments or discoveries:

What is this person most known for:

How would the world be different if he had never been born?

Greatest Explorations:

Design a postage stamp to commemorate this person

Greatest Discoveries:

MATTHEW HENSON

It's Research Time!

Using Internet search, Wikipedia, documentaries or library

Date and place of birth:

What was (or is) his job?

What were (or are) his goals?

What challenges did he face along the way?

Who or what motivated him to accomplish what he did?

Name some of his most notable accomplishments or discoveries:

What is this person most known for:

How would the world be different if he had never been born?

Greatest Explorations:

Design a postage stamp to commemorate this person

Greatest Discoveries:

HENRY HUDSON

It's Research Time!

Using Internet search, Wikipedia, documentaries or library

Date and place of birth:

What was (or is) his job?

What were (or are) his goals?

What challenges did he face along the way?

Who or what motivated him to accomplish what he did?

Name some of his most notable accomplishments or discoveries:

What is this person most known for:

How would the world be different if he had never been born?

Greatest Explorations:

Design a postage stamp to commemorate this person

Greatest Discoveries:

MAE JEMISON

It's Research Time!

Using Internet search, Wikipedia, documentaries or library

Date and place of birth:

What was (or is) her job?

What were (or are) her goals?

What was her main goal?

In what ways did her life affect our world?

What is this person most known for:

How would the world be different if she had never been born?

Greatest Explorations:

Design a postage stamp to commemorate this person

Greatest Discoveries:

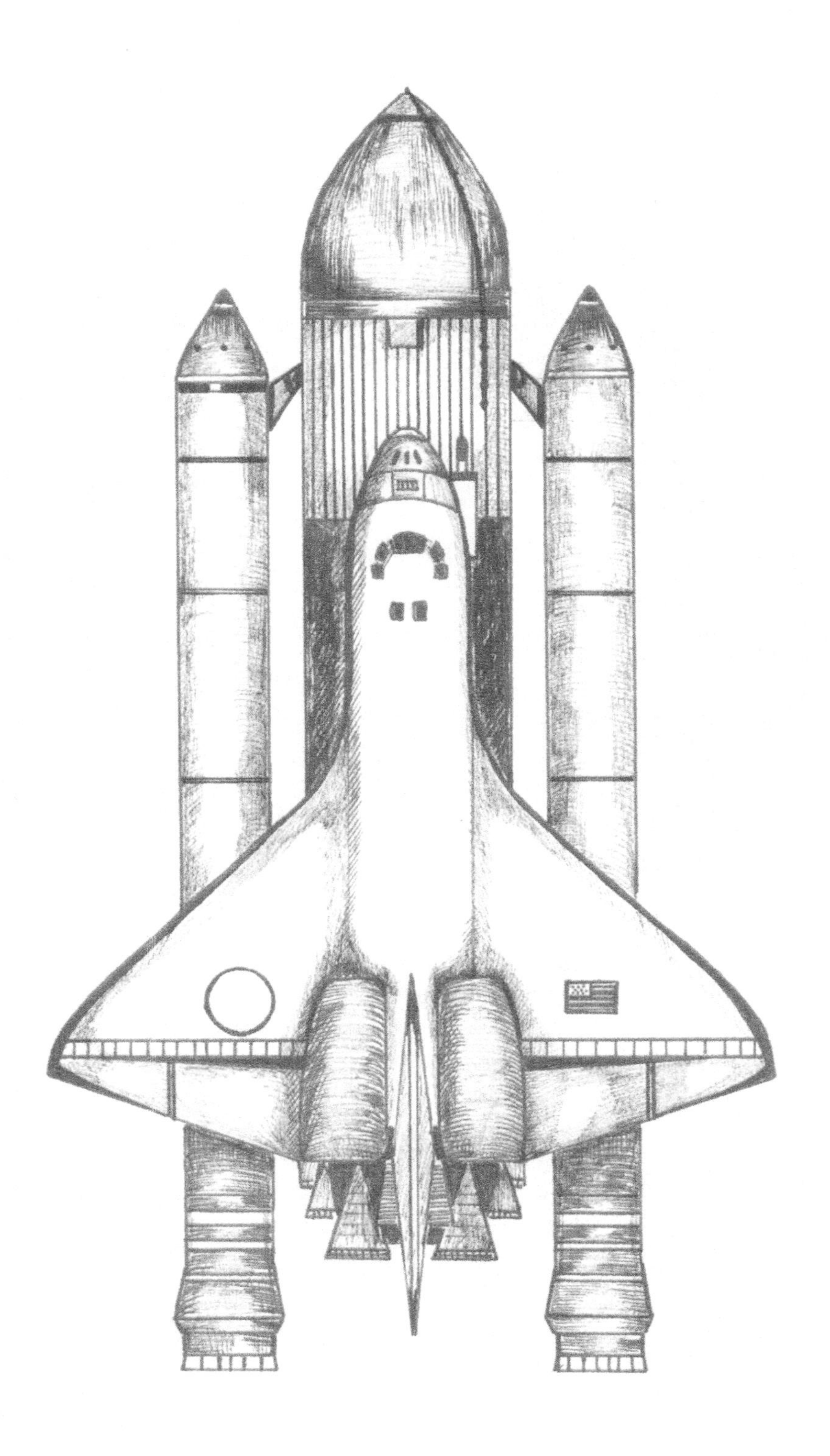

KATHERINE JOHNSON

It's Research Time!

Using Internet search, Wikipedia, documentaries or library

Date and place of birth:

What was (or is) her job?

What were (or are) her goals?

What was her main goal?

In what ways did her life affect our world?

What is this person most known for:

How would the world be different if she had never been born?

Greatest Explorations:

Design a postage stamp to commemorate this person

Greatest Discoveries:

29

GERLINDE KALTENBRUNNER

It's Research Time!

Using Internet search, Wikipedia, documentaries or library

Date and place of birth:

What was (or is) her job?

What were (or are) her goals?

What was her main goal?

In what ways did her life affect our world?

What is this person most known for:

How would the world be different if she had never been born?

Greatest Explorations:

Design a postage stamp to commemorate this person

Greatest Discoveries:

CHRISTINA KOCH

It's Research Time!

Using Internet search, Wikipedia, documentaries or library

Date and place of birth:

What was (or is) her job?

What were (or are) her goals?

What was her main goal?

In what ways did her life affect our world?

What is this person most known for:

How would the world be different if she had never been born?

Greatest Explorations:

Design a postage stamp to commemorate this person

Greatest Discoveries:

CAPT. MERIWETHER LEWIS

It's Research Time!

Using Internet search, Wikipedia, documentaries or library

Date and place of birth:

What was (or is) his job?

What were (or are) his goals?

What challenges did he face along the way?

Who or what motivated him to accomplish what he did?

Name some of his most notable accomplishments or discoveries:

What is this person most known for:

How would the world be different if he had never been born?

Greatest Explorations:

Design a postage stamp to commemorate this person

Greatest Discoveries:

FERDINAND MAGELLAN

It's Research Time!

Using Internet search, Wikipedia, documentaries or library

Date and place of birth:

What was (or is) his job?

What were (or are) his goals?

What challenges did he face along the way?

Who or what motivated him to accomplish what he did?

Name some of his most notable accomplishments or discoveries:

What is this person most known for:

How would the world be different if he had never been born?

Greatest Explorations:

Design a postage stamp to commemorate this person

Greatest Discoveries:

JESSICA MEIR

It's Research Time!

Using Internet search, Wikipedia, documentaries or library

Date and place of birth:

What was (or is) her job?

What were (or are) her goals?

What was her main goal?

In what ways did her life affect our world?

What is this person most known for:

How would the world be different if she had never been born?

Greatest Explorations:

Design a postage stamp to commemorate this person

Greatest Discoveries:

KT MILLER

It's Research Time!

Using Internet search, Wikipedia, documentaries or library

Date and place of birth:

What was (or is) her job?

What were (or are) her goals?

What was her main goal?

In what ways did her life affect our world?

What is this person most known for:

How would the world be different if she had never been born?

Greatest Explorations:

Design a postage stamp to commemorate this person

Greatest Discoveries:

ELON MUSK

It's Research Time!

Using Internet search, Wikipedia, documentaries or library

Date and place of birth:

What was (or is) his job?

What were (or are) his goals?

What challenges did he face along the way?

Who or what motivated him to accomplish what he did?

Name some of his most notable accomplishments or discoveries:

What is this person most known for:

How would the world be different if he had never been born?

Greatest Explorations:

Design a postage stamp to commemorate this person

Greatest Discoveries:

SUNITA PANDYA

It's Research Time!

Using Internet search, Wikipedia, documentaries or library

Date and place of birth:

What was (or is) her job?

What were (or are) her goals?

What was her main goal?

In what ways did her life affect our world?

What is this person most known for:

How would the world be different if she had never been born?

Greatest Explorations:

Design a postage stamp to commemorate this person

Greatest Discoveries:

FRANCISCO PIZARRO

It's Research Time!

Using Internet search, Wikipedia, documentaries or library

Date and place of birth:

What was (or is) his job?

What were (or are) his goals?

What challenges did he face along the way?

Who or what motivated him to accomplish what he did?

Name some of his most notable accomplishments or discoveries:

What is this person most known for:

How would the world be different if he had never been born?

Greatest Explorations:

Design a postage stamp to commemorate this person

Greatest Discoveries:

JEAN BAPTISTE POINTE DU SABLE

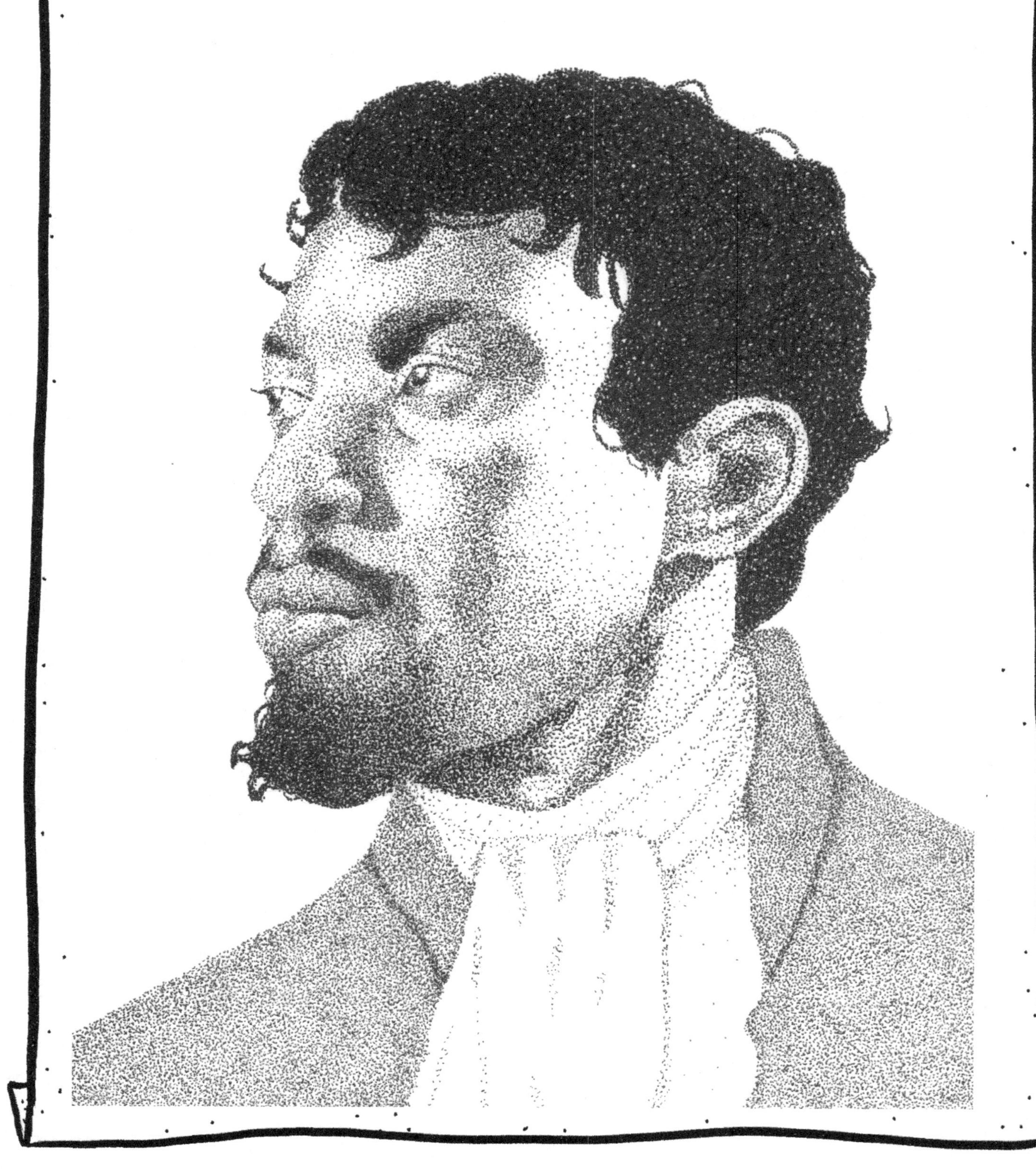

It's Research Time!

Using Internet search, Wikipedia, documentaries or library

Date and place of birth:

What was (or is) his job?

What were (or are) his goals?

What challenges did he face along the way?

Who or what motivated him to accomplish what he did?

Name some of his most notable accomplishments or discoveries:

What is this person most known for:

How would the world be different if he had never been born?

Greatest Explorations:

Design a postage stamp to commemorate this person

Greatest Discoveries:

JUAN PONCE DE LEON

It's Research Time!

Using Internet search, Wikipedia, documentaries or library

Date and place of birth:

What was (or is) his job?

What were (or are) his goals?

What challenges did he face along the way?

Who or what motivated him to accomplish what he did?

Name some of his most notable accomplishments or discoveries:

What is this person most known for:

How would the world be different if he had never been born?

Greatest Explorations:

Design a postage stamp to commemorate this person

Greatest Discoveries:

SACAGAWEA

It's Research Time!

Using Internet search, Wikipedia, documentaries or library

Date and place of birth:

What was (or is) her job?

What were (or are) her goals?

What was her main goal?

In what ways did her life affect our world?

What is this person most known for:

How would the world be different if she had never been born?

Greatest Explorations:

Design a postage stamp to commemorate this person

Greatest Discoveries:

HERNANDO DE SOTO

It's Research Time!

Using Internet search, Wikipedia, documentaries or library

Date and place of birth:

What was (or is) his job?

What were (or are) his goals?

What challenges did he face along the way?

Who or what motivated him to accomplish what he did?

Name some of his most notable accomplishments or discoveries:

What is this person most known for:

How would the world be different if he had never been born?

Greatest Explorations:

Design a postage stamp to commemorate this person

Greatest Discoveries:

AMERIGO VESPUCCI

It's Research Time!

Using Internet search, Wikipedia, documentaries or library

Date and place of birth:

What was (or is) his job?

What were (or are) his goals?

What challenges did he face along the way?

Who or what motivated him to accomplish what he did?

Name some of his most notable accomplishments or discoveries:

What is this person most known for:

How would the world be different if he had never been born?

Greatest Explorations:

Design a postage stamp to commemorate this person

Greatest Discoveries:

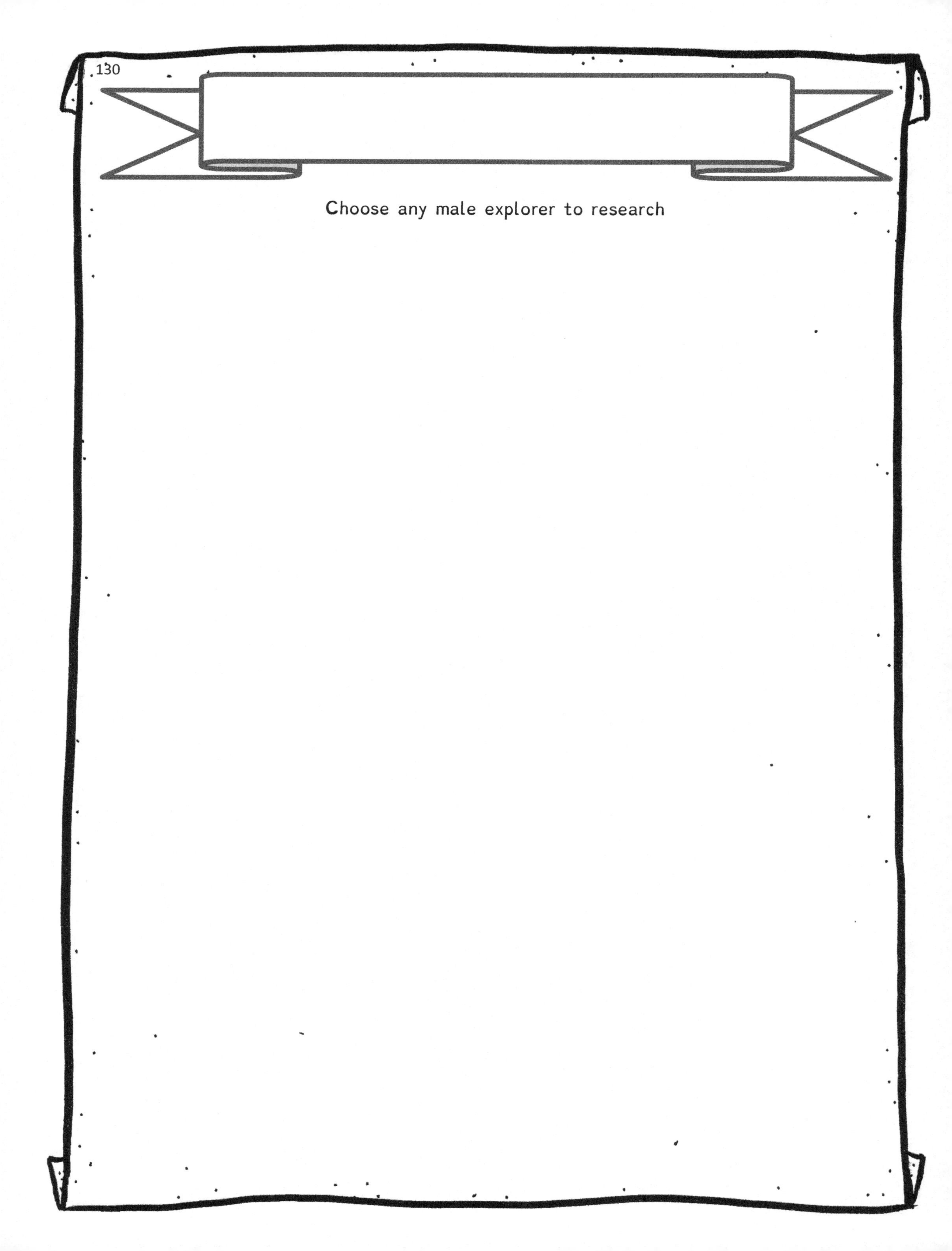
Choose any male explorer to research

It's Research Time!

Using Internet search, Wikipedia, documentaries or library

Date and place of birth:

What was (or is) his job?

What were (or are) his goals?

What challenges did he face along the way?

Who or what motivated him to accomplish what he did?

Name some of his most notable accomplishments or discoveries:

What is this person most known for:

How would the world be different if he had never been born?

Greatest Explorations:

Design a postage stamp to commemorate this person

Greatest Discoveries:

Choose any female explorer to research

It's Research Time!

Using Internet search, Wikipedia, documentaries or library

Date and place of birth:

What was (or is) her job?

What were (or are) her goals?

What was her main goal?

In what ways did her life affect our world?

What is this person most known for:

How would the world be different if she had never been born?

Greatest Explorations:

Design a postage stamp to commemorate this person

Greatest Discoveries:

Choose any male explorer to research

It's Research Time!

Using Internet search, Wikipedia, documentaries or library

Date and place of birth:

What was (or is) his job?

What were (or are) his goals?

What challenges did he face along the way?

Who or what motivated him to accomplish what he did?

Name some of his most notable accomplishments or discoveries:

What is this person most known for:

How would the world be different if he had never been born?

Greatest Explorations:

Design a postage stamp to commemorate this person

Greatest Discoveries:

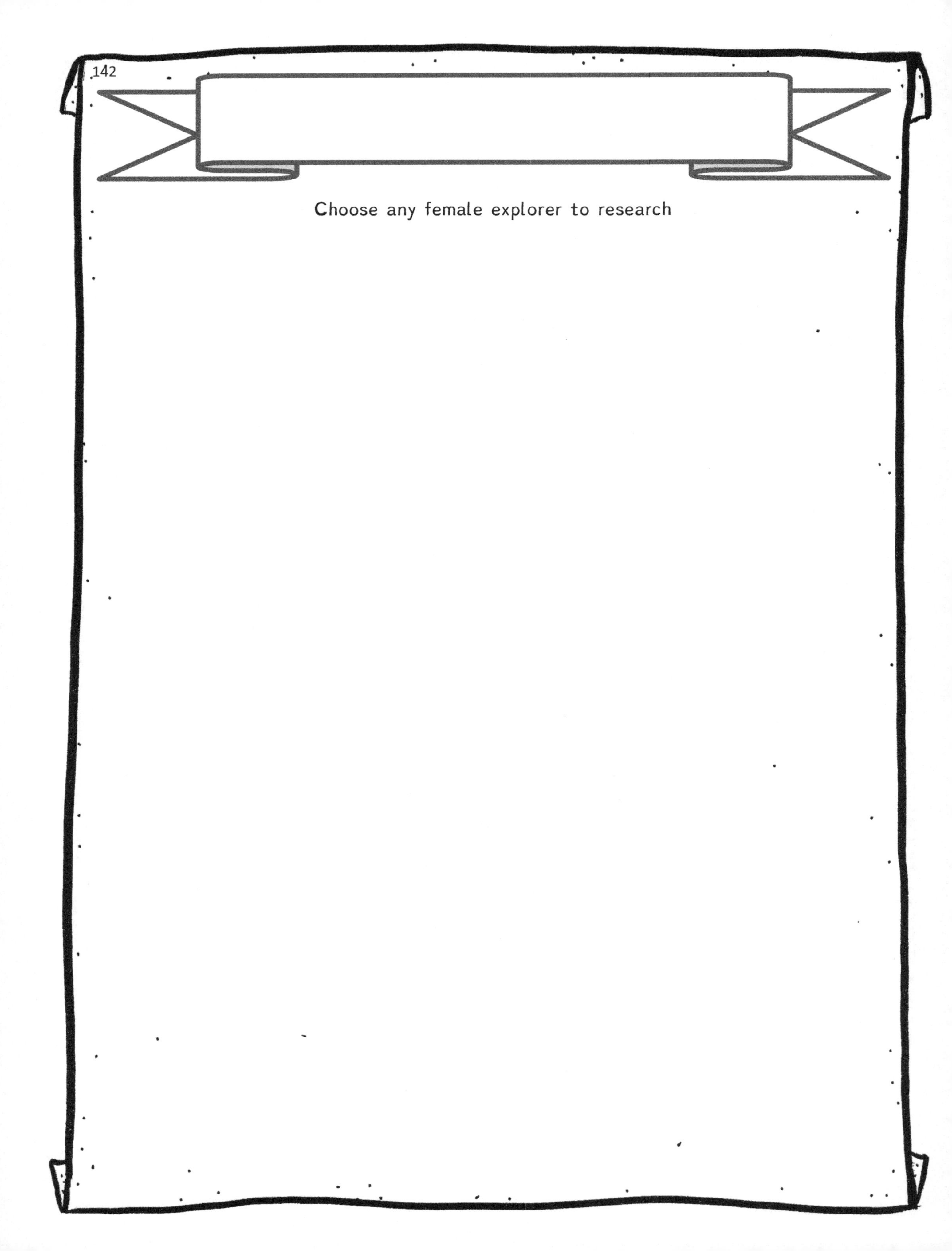
Choose any female explorer to research

It's Research Time!

Using Internet search, Wikipedia, documentaries or library

Date and place of birth:

What was (or is) her job?

What were (or are) her goals?

What was her main goal?

In what ways did her life affect our world?

What is this person most known for:

How would the world be different if she had never been born?

Greatest Explorations:

Design a postage stamp to commemorate this person

Greatest Discoveries:

Resources Used in Research:

Additional Notes:

What Is Fun-Schooling?

Fun-schooling is a one-of-a-kind way to learn. It is tapping into kid's interests while covering all the major subjects. Fun-schooling is for creative learners, students with learning disabilities, gifted students, and everyone in between. It's a way for students to learn without the stress, pressure, and boredom of other methods. We started out creating materials for our children. Then friends and family wanted to try it out. Before we knew it, Fun-schooling with Thinking Tree Books was born!

Fun-Schooling With Thinking Tree Books

Contact Us:

The Thinking Tree LLC

+1 (USA) 317.622.8852

info@funschooling.com

THE Thinking TREE
PUBLISHING COMPANY
Sarah Janisse Brown
ART
LOGIC
SCIENCE
SPELLING
READING
COLOR
THINKING
DRAWING
CREATING

Made in the USA
Coppell, TX
23 May 2022